Sending you joyful hugs this Easter.

May your dreams

and wishes come true.

smile eggs
Happy
Easter
sun
love
HAPPY EGG
life
bunny
joy
good
chicken
spring

Mom & Dad,

Wishing you an Easter that is bright,

happy, and full of contentment.

Hoppy Easter!

Sand-hill Cranes, Robins, and Red winged blackbirds will sing,

Meeting together for the arrival of spring!

Hope your Easter is bright with color,
sweet with treats, and warm with sunshine!

Mom & Dad,

May the hope of spring

bring days that are filled with joy,

laughter, and good-times!

Easter wishes that are as sweet and

special as you both!

Easter is more than just eggs and candy.

It is also about peace, love, and family.

Mom & Dad,

I'm thinking about you both...

Have a wonderful bunny day!

Delivering hugs, kisses,
and Easter wishes!

Thinking of you this season of renewal
& wishing you happiness at
Easter & throughout the year.

Here's hoping your spring is filled with
the beauty of nature.

Mom & Dad,

May your Easter holiday bring you health, happiness, and lots of love!

from Florabella Publishing, LLC

www.ingramcontent.com/pod-product-compliance
Lightning Source LLC
Chambersburg PA
CBHW061925270726
48659CB00002BA/931